ANGER: A
HEALTHY EMOTION

Dr.Eden Payam Fazel
MD,MSc,Dip Coaching

For Barack Obama, and the fresh fragrance of new peace in our troubled world.

And for all refugees who perish from nostalgia in exile, from Ishmael the black diamond and first son of Abraham and his legitimate black wife Hagar, up to this day.

تقدیم به ... اکبر نیک نژاد

و صداقت ریشه ی قلم هایش

(signature)

About Eden and "Survive and thrive"

Eden initially trained as a medical doctor specialising in preventive medicine and public mental health and later qualified as an individual and organisational Coach. Having worked in 31 countries across Africa, Asia, Europe and the Middle East as a medical trainer, organisational coach, and aid worker, he constantly remained curious to learn from every culture, lifestyle and tradition.

Eden soon realised that conventional medicine doesn't have the answers to all problems and that we need to resort to the nature within us and the nature without to survive and thrive. Having been through various stretching life challenges, Eden survived and thrived, now sharing his experience with others.

He carried out extensive research into the natural behaviour of man and animals, to find out who we are, where we come from and what is the natural life style, that suits us best.

Eden is based in Hebden Bridge and travels across the UK and Europe to deliver his workshops to groups and organisations.

ANGER: A VERY HEALTHY EMOTION

Dr.Eden Payam Fazel
MD,MSc,Dip Coaching

Our emotions are our sixth
sense, the vital powers that
interpret, arrange, direct, and
summarise the other five.
Emotions tell us whether what
we experience is threatening,
hurtful, regretful, sad or
delightful.
When feelings speak, we can
only listen – and sometimes
act – even if we don't always
want to understand why. Not
to be aware of our emotions,
not to appreciate, interpret
and know how to express them
is worse than being blind
or paralysed. Not to feel is
nothing less than death. More

than anything else emotions make us human. Anger is one of those emotions. We should come close to it, make friends with it and make it work for us!

In his very interesting book the psychopathology of human destructiveness, Eric Fromm says:

Anger is the feeling of being irritated, miffed, teed-off, irked, annoyed, furious, enraged, "burned".

People get angry when they have been hurt, and so everyone has angry feelings from time to time. When a person tells you he never gets angry, he is really telling you he doesn't recognise his anger or is concealing it because he is afraid of what it may reveal about him.

You don't have to be seething with rage to qualify as being angry. Indeed, most of the anger that people feel is not violent or difficult to control. It is irritation or annoyance, the usual response to every day disappointments.

How does anger result from being hurt? Any emotional injury drains your energy by creating a negative feeling that has to be resolved in some way. The natural reaction is to redirect the negative feeling outside you,

at whatever caused the pain.
This is the most effective
way of settling anger, but it
is not quite as simple as it
seems, because the cause of
the hurt is not always clearly
identifiable.

Expressing anger over the
hurt that causes it allows an
emotional injury to heal.
If any loss is to heal in
the best way, the anger it
generates needs to be allowed
full freedom of expression.
The first step in repairing an
injury is to make the hurt
known by getting angry.
The second is to direct that
anger towards an appropriate
target. Expressing anger is

a natural, healthy response and is necessary to keep one's emotions in balance.

This isn't to say that anger is a pleasant feeling. There is a great deal of stress involved as one's blood pressure climbs and heart rate accelerates. But if the angry person can release the emotional and physical tension that has built up inside, he will eventually feel better.

Trouble comes when the true source of the hurt is unavailable to get angry at or when do so causes so much unacceptable pain the anger is blocked and the angry feelings fester inside.

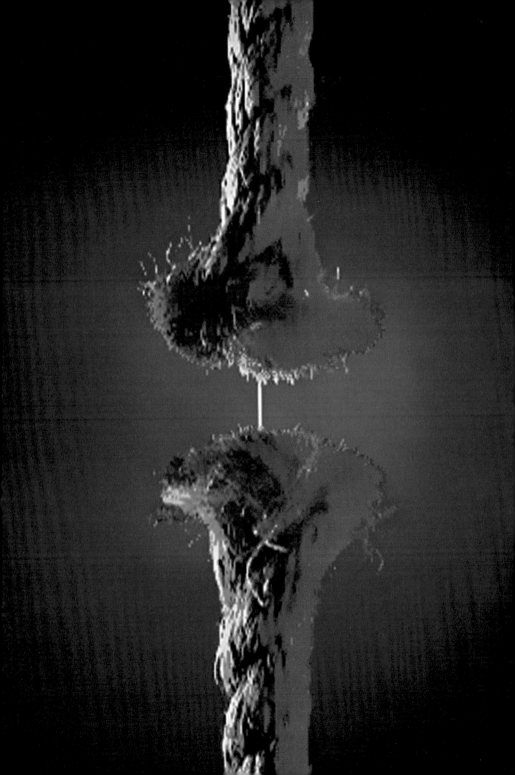

Some people feel that it's wrong to be angry and refuse to admit to even the mildest annoyance. Others dislike getting angry because it is unpleasant. Some people mistakenly believe it will just go away if they ignore it, or are afraid that if they get angry they'll lose control, create a scene, embarrass themselves or hurt others. Whatever the reasons people give for not getting angry they are self-deceiving. You can never justify burying your anger.

To hold anger back only adds to the hurt that caused it. The defence that prevent the anger from flowing naturally outward now channel it inward, directing it against you. Someone always pays for anger. Far better it be the one who caused the pain than the one who received it. When you hold anger in, you only punish yourself.

How much anger needs to be expressed to balance hurt? It varies from person to person. Some can merely mention their hurt to the person who caused it and their anger is over and done with. Others have so much pent up anger that they can go in to a rage at getting a wrong number. Of course it is never possible to have a perfect balance between anger and hurt. That would mean one particular loss could be cancelled by one particular feeling. Allowing the anger to flow cleanses the emotional wound and initiates healing.

Some people fear admitting hurt because they don't want to appear weak. Ironically their unaccepted hurt and unexpressed anger over it undermine them and only make them feel less strong, less able to admit future hurt, setting up a vicious cycle that eventually shuts out reality.

Although showing anger is

necessary to balance a hurt,
it is sometimes difficult to
know what is "appropriate".
For example, how can you
possibly express your anger
appropriately at a loved one
who has just died from a long
and painful illness? Is it
appropriate to complain to the
heavens for making the loved
one of such fragile substance?
Is it appropriate to curse the
deceased for his physical
short comings or his neglect
in not seeing his doctors
sooner? Such angry feelings
even if justified are difficult
to admit when the person who
caused them is dead.
You feel guilty getting

angry at someone who's already paid the greatest price. Nonetheless we often are angry at the loved one who has died and left us, however irrational or inappropriate it may be. Then how do we express our anger over such a loss?

This process of releasing anger by directing it outward in an appropriate way is central to the whole issue of hurt and anger. If anger isn't expressed but is defensively held inside, it begins to destroy the person it lives in, eroding everything that feels good in that person. Yet some people seem to be angry all the time and are still irritable and edgy. Why aren't they well-balanced and happy? After all, they are always letting their angry feelings out. Or are they?

Just because a person acts angry doesn't mean that he is settling a hurt in a way that allows him to come to terms with it.

Chronically angry people often blame others for their problems. They seldom receive what they think they deserve. They don't realise that few people in life get much of anything without working for it. But to admit this would require that the person

accept some of the blame for
his own failure. Usually this
is too frightening because it
opens the flood gates:
"If I'm at fault for some of
my failures, maybe I'm
at fault for all of them."
This is too depressing and
overwhelming to contemplate;
more comfortable to guard
against any attempt at
self blame by continually
directing anger outward – an
anger that becomes a defense
and indeed a way of life.
Any passing slight adds to
the reservoir of pain. Anger
is continually discharged
–scatter shot – without ever
coming to grips with the

original source of hurt.
Confusion, frustration and
escalating bitterness
result- searching for
a target that can't or doesn't
want to be located.
The direct appropriate
expression of anger, on the
other hand, is a necessary
part of a healthy emotional
life. Don't regret having
angry feelings. Everyone
gets angry when they get
hurt. The only people who
don't get hurt and therefore
angry are those who claim to
have no vulnerabilities. And
people with no vulnerabilities
have no sensitivity.
They also can't respond to

another's feelings or share,
or be intimate, because they
have no access to their own
feelings.

Sometimes when a hurt is
relatively slight a person
may bury it rather than
express it in anger. This can
become a bad habit, because
many small silent hurts
can add up to produce a big
anger. When that happens
no single cause of the pain
seems important enough to
justify getting as angry as
the person now feels.

To let out that much anger
at any of the little wounds
would seem inappropriate,
so it is held in. Which is the

way to disaster.

When angry feelings are allowed to flow naturally to wherever they appropriately lead, what happens? The answer is different for everyone has his own style and personality, and so each hurt feels different accordingly. But basically once the matter is confronted openly, and honestly, the anger once out, is out.

The slate is clear again! Difficulties occur when people try to modify their natural feelings to make them more acceptable to others. In so doing they vent only part of the anger still feel trapped.

Nothing adds to a person's sense of frustration as much as trapped anger. The person who truly understands his feelings doesn't sit and brood in silence over pain, constructing angry fantasies of retaliation. Instead he openly confronts the person who hurt him and as quickly as possible tells him exactly what he thinks of the situation with as little fanfare or exaggeration as possible. He does not rub the other person's nose in his misdeed, nor does he play the role of the injured party who now has a right not merely to retaliate but also to humiliate.

People who act out their
fantasies of revenge don't
merely want to get even,
but to destroy. Admitting
that you feel this angry
is a good first step toward
finding the proper perspective.
Many people are reluctant
to get angry because their
fantasies are so violent they
frighten and confuse them.
They worry they'd really go
overboard if they let lose and
prove to the world that they
are the monsters. They don't
realise that their fantasies
are the result of holding back
itself. So they do nothing.
But these alternatives,
overreacting and not reacting

at all, are unhealthy.
There are better ways of
releasing anger. Here are
some points to remember;
When someone has hurt you
tell them so - directly and
openly -..."you hurt me"...and
also tell them exactly why.
Do this is in private. Don't
unnecessarily set on the
defensive. It will only make
them feel like retaliating
rather than listening. Be
firm as you need to be to
get your point across but
try not to be punitive. If the
person denies he hurt you,
point out the facts again
and say you know what
you feel. If the other person

tells you are too sensitive, that he was just kidding, point out that people vary in their sensitivity – one man's kidding is another man's pain. Tell him you want to make him aware of you sensitivities so that he can take them into consideration in future. If you feel the other person hurt you on purpose, say so. When people hurt others intentionally they often do so out of anger. If this is the case, ask that he be more direct in expressing his anger next time, telling you the problem without causing unnecessary hurt. When someone hurts you

like this, it is up to you to act in control, the other person is already acting childish. Retaliating seldom solves the problem and often obscures the point that both parties are trying to make. It causes guilt, pushes people apart and wastes time and energy. Expressing anger properly is healthy and restoring, but there are many people who can't seem to handle anger at all. Feeling angry makes them feel bad about themselves, and so they keep their feelings bottled up. People fear getting angry for different reasons, depending, to some degree, on their background and past experiences. Dependent people are afraid they being angry will prove they are unlovable. They are afraid that expressing their anger will turn away the people they need for nurturing and support. Many of these people had difficulty in being nurtured as children, and grew up with a feeling of insecurity over their own worth as a person. Such people have learned to swallow most of their anger and often feel trapped, helpless and empty. When they do get angry they are often inappropriate in their choice of target and out

of control. Their rage may
be directed at a "safe" target,
such as a helpless child – just
like themselves. Many child
beaters are in this category.
People who felt unloved in
childhood almost never feel
uncomfortable getting angry
at someone they love. Instead
they may act helpless or
beaten as a way of getting
to others. It' as if they were
saying, "See, look what you
are making me do to myself."
Their approach almost never
works – they only succeed in
pushing the people they need
further away from them.
Dependent people go through
life struggling angrily

and half heartedly for their independence. They may feel someone is holding them back, not giving them what they are entitled to. Their anger is very much like a child's who feels mistreated and wants to get even but doesn't know how. Because their goals tend to be so dependent on, they don't make the effort for themselves where it counts. Their anger is turned in on themselves, and their anger is quickly dissipated.

As for the controlling people, they tend to equate showing anger with losing control. They try to warn off hurts

and anger by elaborate
mental manipulations.
But feelings simply can't
be controlled as they'd like.
Feelings want to be expressed.
Trying to control them
merely reshapes the
way they may appear
but it doesn't change the
feeling itself or diminish
it's impact. People who are
especially interested in
control seem always to be
looking for excuses for their
feelings. They intellectualise,
rationalise, project, isolate
and otherwise confuse the
real issues. They hardly ever
see anything in a simple or
uncomplicated way. For a

controlling person to say,
"You hurt me and I am
angry with you", is very
difficult. To be vulnerable, for
them is to be out of control.
Anger is a powerful feeling,
and to channel it away
from emotional expression
by intellectual events and
feelings that you often forget
what the hurt was about. The
first step in settling anger,
the admission of the hurt,
becomes the first stumbling
block that controlling people
need to overcome. It is doubly
hard for them because,
although they can easily talk
about their feelings in words,
the words don't translate

in to emotions.

Not only do they have a difficult time expressing anger, they also find it exceedingly painful to accept proper responsibility for another person. If you get angry at a controlling person for hurting you, you may find it an especially unrewarding experience. When you make your point the controlling person will probably give you a detailed explanation to prove his actions were out of the best intentions. The fault is yours. The hurt inflicted on you wasn't really a hurt at all, but your own

shortcoming finally brought
to life by his generous
behaviour that, of course, was
for your own good. Confused?
You are supposed to be.
Controlling people can
be difficult to deal with
because they are simply
so intellectually involved
and so far removed from
their feelings that they
aren't really honest. Worse
than that, they have a
limited ability to accept
their dishonesty and so
give defensive excuses
when concerned. They see
themselves as people who
must be perfect and use
their formidable defences

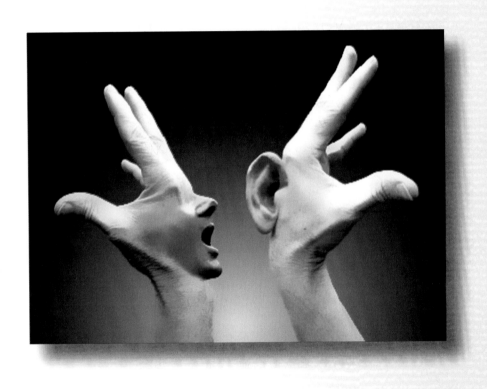

to lure you away from any
meaningful discussion of
their feelings, their anger, or
their weak points.

When these people do show
anger, it is extraordinarily
unpleasant. One has the
feeling of being in the same
room with a mad tyrant.
They are unable to say
simply, "You hurt me".
Their anger is so tied up in
intellectualised defences
that it is never really free
to be expressed simply and
directly. Instead, they lash
out in torrents of rage. Such
people need to learn express
their anger a little at a
time and, most of all, come

to realise that they can be angry without losing control – without going to pieces. People most worried about esteem and superficial appearances often suppress their anger by hiding behind an act of some kind. By exaggerating their reactions they deny their real feelings. For example, they may act wildly, hysterically angry, but when asked about it won't admit anything is really wrong. "I was only pretending", they will say. Such people would rather play the role of an angry person than admit to their real feelings of anger. To reveal their own feelings forthrightly is to risk being judged. Instead of risking the loss of your respect or admiration, they disguise their anger. Their feelings often manifest themselves as physical complaints. Everyone is familiar, for example with headaches caused by held in anger – "I've got one of my 'sick headaches,' " goes the refrain, instead of, "I'd like to kick you in the teeth," which may feel closer to the anger felt. By masking real feelings these physical symptoms spare the person from being judged and rejected

for being angry
(and hence being "bad").
Another way these people
handle anger is to "split off"
any angry outbursts from
themselves as if it didn't
belong to them at all. Later
they may conveniently
forget the outbursts and
refuse to accept the anger as
their own. The problem with
managing anger that way
is that it uses up so much
energy, wears you out, and
the anger is never really
directed at those who caused
it. The people who are to blame
aren't even put on notice
they've been hurtful.
The injured person hasn't

directly defended or expressed himself, and so there is no relief from the cycle of hurt and anger.

Some of us have large reservoirs of anger that require all our energy to handle. Such a backlog of unresolved feelings needs to be decreased to levels where we begin to have energy available for investing in the real world outside. It is difficult to react to the world in a fairly easy, outgoing manner if you continually feel anxious that you are going to lose control and blow up.

When you are filled with

negative feelings, you may be ready to battle at the drop of a hat, not to mention a word or a look. Some days are like that for everyone, of course. There are days when something goes wrong that is hard to identify, and so we go through the day being irritable and snippy, looking for people to get in to arguments with and being generally unpleasant. But to live one's whole life this way is intolerable.

In the traditional ways of psychotherapy, people with such long standing painful feelings are led back in to their pasts to uncover the

source of the original pain
and then come to terms with
it. The theory is that the
person, now older and wiser
and having the perspective
of many years growth and
much suffering, will be able
to view the old pain with a
new distance and accuracy
and so be better able to put
away his old defensive
devices for dealing with that
pain, this method doesn't
always work so simply and
neatly in practice. Just to
grow up is to gain a new
perspective on past hurts,
successes, loves and hates so
we can see the present more in
keeping with what is

and less with what was.
The best way to change
one's perspective on the past
is to deal honestly with the
feelings of the present and
to resolve those feelings as
completely as possible as they
occur. If you are angry, show
it. Don't take refuge in a
headache. Don't pretend you
are above such feelings. And
don't try to ignore them and
bury them in the past.
Every therapeutic process
takes place in the present,
whether or not the events
being discussed are from
the present or the past. What
you should ultimately learn
in any form of therapy is a

better way of discharging feelings so that the minimal residue remains from emotional encounters and you are free to interact without emotional legacies. The best way to change your attitude toward the past is to become as honest as possible in the present. Being totally honest is the best way to live in any case. Existing at levels of lesser honesty takes up too much energy and always relies on defences. You can't live your life telling lies- especially to yourself. Becoming totally honest is the first step to becoming free.

Expressing your feelings openly is the second.

Other people may feel you are overdoing it the first time you express strong feelings such as anger openly. Just remember that most people avoid making any kind of disturbance – "don't make waves," we are told – and your anger, even if it's mild, will appear unusual. Some people will be startled or upset by your honesty. That is too bad. You just try to speak out with the truth as you see it. Most people worth getting angry at –people you care about will accept or at least tolerate your new attitude.

Those who won't, don't respect your right to be a person.

It may take some months for you to feel natural expressing your feelings, especially anger. When you first begin to be open, you may feel your emotions build and rush to the surface, almost sweeping you away with them. It is tempting to close down and rein them in again. Be brave. Don't hold back. Let them out. The process of learning to express feelings is painful. It requires your determination. Stick with it. It will pay off as trapped feelings of hurt and anger form the past come out and escape piggyback on their counterpart feelings of the present. Now you'll no longer feel as if you must always be on guard to hold back forbidden feelings. As you become more accustomed to being open, you'll b amazed at how little time and energy it takes to keep current with your feelings. Saying, "you hurt me," will literally become a matter of course. People who are dishonest will find it more difficult to deal with you and will keep their distance – for which you can be grateful. Life will be fuller and richer because there will

be more of you available for
the people and things you love
in the present.

In time another important
thing will happen: the
feelings you now hold in
aren't your feelings from the
long-forgotten past of early
childhood, but the feelings
of present, everyday life.
The angers of this week,
yesterday, this morning are
now culprits. Not large hurts,
but little events insult and
hurt you everyday. It is your
faulty pattern of dealing
with feelings on a day to
day basis that causes most
of the difficulty in your life
and it can be recognised and

adjusted without hauling out
all the heavy baggage of the
past. The process of growth
and becoming is continuous.
If we are open to it, it can
offer new opportunities to
find ourselves and reshape
the course of our lives. Just
as adolescence offers new
opportunities to re-examine
the issues of independence,
control, esteem and identity,
the remaining years of
our lives present chances to
redefine ourselves, to seek
our freedom and learn to be
ourselves without apology.
Again, the secret to success
in this continuum of growth
is to be honest with your

feelings at all times. Every time you are dishonest you create a problem, reinforce a negative energy or bolster an old defensive system which then distorts reality and interferes with your ability to cope with the real world.

If You are hurt and don't experience the expected anger, ask yourself why not. Where has the anger gone? Are you hiding it? Are you pretending it doesn't bother you? Why shouldn't you feel angry when you are hurt? Are you afraid of appearing vulnerable in front of a particular person? When you are afraid of opening

up in front of a particular
person but have been able
to do so with others, it may
mean you don't really trust
that person. You are afraid
that exposing yourself to
him would be a risk. He
might hurt you further or
retaliate. Tell him that if
your natural expression of
a feeling is blocked by the
presence of another person,
that person is keeping you
from being honest and free.
The inhibitions you may
feel may actually be his
defences, working to shut
you off. Pointing out how
his presence inhibits you and
makes it difficult for you to

be your best and most honest
self is your best weapon
and most valuable insight.
Avoiding people who enhance
or encourage your dishonesty
is probably a good idea. It is
hard enough being honest
without inviting situations
that bring out the
worst in you.
Of course, there are times
when expressing anger
creates problems. Everyone is
familiar with the demanding
and unappreciative employer
who treats employees like
objects making them feel
insignificant, constantly
hurting them and using his
authority to intimidate them.

The employees feel irritable and defensive and tend to perceive the boss negatively even when he has no negative intention. Expressing anger in a situation carries it's complications. Not the least of which is losing your job. If you have an employer like this you have a choice – you can learn to accept his negative ways without becoming personally involved, or you can change jobs.

But of course that's not always as easy as it sounds. Many people feel trapped in a job out of fear of change or because they don't want to lose their seniority. The protective structure provided by seniority and unions is remarkably analogous to our psychological defensive systems. Originally they were constructed to keep us from being vulnerable and protect us from possible hurt. Then we became dependent on them and found it hard to function without them. We have a way of recreating in our immediate environment the same problems and patterns that imprison us in our own minds.

It's true that the way our present society is constructed, even when we become free of our own defences, our openness tends to bring us in to some conflict with the defences and controlling patterns of the world we are trying to survive in. Still, there is always room for increasing the openness and access to your own feelings and to the feelings of others. That is the real world, the one most accessible, most rewarding and over which you can assert the maximum healthy control for you own good.

Often the people we become angry at are people without faces or names, people who pass by so quickly we hardly notice them- the bus driver who slams the door in our face, the police officer with a chip on his shoulder, the nasty waitress, the irritable ticket taker, the obnoxious cab driver, the authoritative lawyer, the pompous doctor. All hurt us in ways that make us angry, but we need the services and assistance of these people and are forced to endure their negative manner and hostile attitudes.

But how to deal with anger created by people like this? The doctor will often become defensive and arrogant when confronted. The lawyer will find some way of getting back at you that you will undoubtedly pay dearly for. In the best of worlds it should be possible to simply tell the person he has hurt you. But many of these people don't really care. What then? To take affront at these episodes and make them a personal issue is the worst thing you can do. You end up wasting a great deal of energy and gain very little. Still, even in these situations the moment may come when you can usefully give your opinion of their behaviour straightforwardly and honestly. Tell the cab driver when you pay him that you felt he was rude and therefore you are not tipping him. Tell the person who is surly to you, "You have a chip on your shoulder, and I'm not going to knock it off."

Again, the important thing is to let it be their problem, not yours. Be thankful that your own feelings are settled in ways that leave you human. Aren't you glad you aren't the bus driver, being so angry all the time? If someone wilfully hurts you, it is their problem, but to let them gain control over your feelings and make you angry for the entire day, that is your problem. The best way

of dealing with such people is to be in tune with your own feelings – if you are, these people can't easily push you over into an angry mood. Letting anger out as you feel it makes all the difference in the world.

Protesting is standing up for yourself. Protesting is defending your beliefs, your boundaries. It is a declaration that you will Not permit trespass. The purpose of displaying anger when you are hurt is to define the limits of your toleration and make your point with force so that no one will mistake your intentions. It is an affirmation of strength and survival.

All creatures give warnings when they are injured or threatened. Your capacity to protest may have been inhibited by your fear of rejection or the politics of your family structure that convinced you that protesting was impolite, ungentlemanly, or unladylike. Raising your voice may have been regarded as uncouth or disrespectful. In spite of what you have been taught, there is actually great therapeutic value in protesting - specially - when someone you love has hurt you. The value of remaining silent in the face of injury from a loved one is hard to defend. If you say nothing when you are hurt, the consequences are horrendous, for nothing destroys your love for another person like harbouring resentment.

The reason you are hurt by another person is that they gave hurt, insulted, offended, or disappointed you. In the face of these negative feelings, is it pure self-deception to claim that you actively feel love for them! What you are really saying is that you remember feeling love for them and that you probably will love them when the hostility between you decreases, but right now you do not!

Protesting is a powerful and emotionally redemptive act, if you make your protests at the right time and to the right person. You must rise to the disputes of your heart. You must make your emotional case. You must go into battle with the person who torments you!

What do you risk when you protest?

You risk discovering that the other person does not love you or care about your feelings. You risk discovering that

you were mistaken.
You risk hurting other
people's feelings. You risk
proving to others that you
don't care, that you are
disobedient or disrespectful.
You risk being humiliated or
ignored. But if you
do not protest:
Others will not know what
you feel or what matters
to you.
Others will not know they
have trespassed and will more
than likely do so again.
You will not clear the air.
You will not resolve your
injury when it occurs, which
is the best time to make your
case, to be heard, believed and

taken seriously.

If you don't protest, how on earth will others know they have hurt you? They will have had no warning to keep them from hurting you again. If they do hurt you again, even if it is not intentional, you will be convinced they meant to hurt you and you will be more likely to overreact. Filled with mistaken resolve, you'll end up doing the most damage.

Go on, protest! Tell the other person how you feel.

Dispute your injury; speak up when you are hurt.

You may be surprised to find that the injury was just a

mistake! Be willing to accept apologies and let go. Just be aware that if you are new to speaking up, you run the risk of unleashing old anger when you do so. So try not to overreact, and be gentle to yourself.

NINE EXCERCISES FOR EXPRESSING ANGER INDIRECTLY

Even if it is too threatening to express your anger directly, you still need to get it out. Although the following nine methods may seem removed and a bit wacky, they can be very helpful.

1.ANGRY LETTERS.

Write a letter to each person
you are angry with.
Begin as follows:
"I am angry with you"
List your complaints as
completely as possible,
but take the time to make
them sensible. You want
the recipient to understand
you, not merely to see you
as ranting and raving. Put
each letter in its own envelope
and place them where you can
easily see them.
Later, if you feel any
additional anger, reread
the pertinent letter and add
the feeling to it. If you have

already made that point,
remind yourself that your
anger is in the letter, outside
you. It is a good idea to
use a bright red envelope to
visualise your anger at a
distance. Keep each letter for
a few weeks or as long as you
feel relief when you look at it.
If after a time you decide
to mail the letter, read
it through several times
consider: Will the person you
are sending it to read it?
Will it cause more harm
than good?
Are your points exaggerated?
Anger that is been held in for
a while tends to blow things
up out of proportion.

2.SAFE ANGRY ACTS.

Write the name of the person you are angry with in large letters on a piece of paper. Expressing yourself with your hands, tear the paper into as many pieces as you can. The quicker you tear the better.

Burn the scraps, thinking, "you deserve my anger" or throw them into the toilet before using it.

This may sound crude, but it works. Repeat as necessary.

Remind yourself of what you have done whenever you see this person.

3.TAKING ANGRY STEPS.

Write the person's name on the sole of your shoe.
All day long, remind yourself that it is there.
Take the delight in getting rid of the anger with every scrape and step you take.

4.ACTING OUT THE ANGER.

Close yourself in a room and scream your worst opinion of this person. It helps to beat with your fists at the same time. Don't be afraid to get worked up.

If you find that this makes you more agitated, try getting even more angry at the pillow and screaming louder and longer, for at least **10** to **15** minutes. The chances are that the screaming and pounding have opened some old feelings and you have to let more out before you feel better. Don't be afraid, even if you begin to cry.

Letting the anger out won't hurt you. When you have completed this, sit quietly for ten minutes and let go.

Wash your face and hands and go for a walk.

Repeat in a few days if necessary.

5. GYM EXERCISES.

Put on a pair of punching
bag gloves. Imagine that the
punching bag is the object
of your anger and let go.
Keep repeating 'This for you!'
Finish with an extended
flurry of punches that
exhausts you.
Say 'it is out.
I feel better,' when you
are done.

6. PARTIAL CONTACT

Pick up the phone and dial
the number of the person you
are angry with.
When your party answers,

push down the buttons to break the connection and start your tirade, pretending the other person on the line. Make sure you keep the button down.

Hearing the other person's voice is an excellent stimulus to provoke your hurt and anger and bring it to the surface.

7. PSYCHODRAMA TECHNIQUES.

Imagine the person you want to tell off is sitting in an empty chair. Tell him exactly how you feel about what he's done to you. Then

sit in the chair and speak to
him, giving his argument
or lame excuses. Then stand
up and discredit him. If you
want witnesses, put other
chairs around and imagine
particular people in each
one. Embarrass that person.
Mortify him.

Go back and forth, playing
you and playing him,
playing witnesses who agree
with you.

Tear his reasoning to pieces.
(You can have your tape
recorder running when you
do this or any of the other
exercises and play the tape
when-ever you want a little
relief.)

8. SYMBOLIC MENIAL TASKS.

Allow your anger to find expression in the positive menial tasks that consume your energy. Cleaning the attic, the cellar, or the garage are all excellent examples. The feeling expressed in the work should be one of purification. Boring, repetitious work is an excellent vehicle for expressing feelings.
The ritual of tedious work can do wonders for setting you straight.
Baptise each weed in your garden with the name of

the person you are angry
with and then weed with a
vengeance.

You can invent your
own exercise, keeping in
mind that you should do
something to get your anger
out, making sure that you do
no harm to another
person or property.

Causing damage only
invalidates the expression
of your anger by
creating a feeling
of remorse. Driving a car
fast is suicidal and
endangers perfect strangers,
many of whom would gladly
sympathise with your cause
if they knew you.

9.RIDICULOUS IMAGERY:

Imagine the person who has offended you dressed in ridiculous disguises, such as red tights and feathers. Or imagine him at a state banquet, nude and eating with his fingers.
A ridiculous fantasy helps dissipate anger nicely and will put a smile on your face that will drive the other person absolutely crazy.
Besides, the other person is already wearing a ridiculous disguise by being an angry person. Your fantasy will help you out that into perspective.

You are the butt of jokes
because you are teasable,
because you permit others
to tease you. Growing up is
to know that you always
have a choice. You need to
learn to take a little distance
and realise that others are
not really bad, but will use
whoever lets them to use them.
Unless you need attention
that badly, you can usually
get out of their way.
You have better things to do
than worry about
getting even!
But be careful, these
devices can become ends in
themselves and should only
be used as a substitute

for the real thing when the actual person is unavailable or you haven't worked up the courage and ability to confront him directly.

Finding Your Gift and Writing your Action Plan

Are you living the life that is right for you?

SURVIVE AND THRIVE
WORKSHOPS

Keys to hardiness, resilience and coherence

Are you best fit to Survive and Thrive in the face of adversity?

SURVIVE AND THRIVE
WORKSHOPS

Negotiation & assertiveness in volatile contexts

Learn to protest now not to become a doormat forever!

SURVIVE AND THRIVE
WORKSHOPS

DiY Counselling,
DiY Coaching

Why don't you do
it yourself?

Biophilia

Learning from natural man and animals: lessons from Ethology

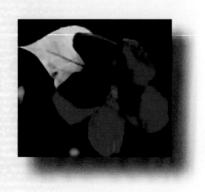

SURVIVE AND THRIVE
WORKSHOPS

Anger a very healthy emotion!

Making friends with anger and making it work for you

Taking good risks

The art of risking: assess, prepare, commit and complete good risks!

SURVIVE AND THRIVE
WORKSHOPS

Knowing your
blind spots

Explore your
strengths and
weaknesses

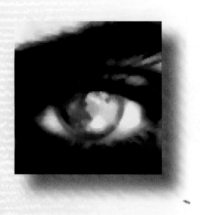

Please contact us through our
website to attend our workshops

Email: surviveandthrive@doctors.net.uk
Website: www.surviveandthrivecoach.org.uk